STUCK ON TH
PRESIDENTS

Cover illustration by **Jonathan Milne**

Sticker art by **Kathie Kelleher**

Written by **Lara Bergen, Lisa Hopp, and Angela Tung**

 Published by Grosset & Dunlap, a division of Penguin Putnam Books for Young Readers, New York. GROSSET & DUNLAP is a registered trademark of Penguin Putnam Inc. Printed in the USA. ISBN 0-448-41284-5
A B C D E F G H I J

THE PRESIDENTIAL OATH OF OFFICE

"I do solemnly swear
that I will faithfully execute
the office of President of the United States,
and will to the best of my ability,
preserve, protect, and defend
the Constitution of the United States."

In more than 200 years, only 43 people have gotten to recite these words. What did they all have in common? They all had the same title: **President of the United States**. Some were born in mansions, others in log cabins. Some went to fancy schools. Others taught themselves to read. But they were all elected to do the same job: lead the country.

The job of the president is many jobs rolled into one:

- As **Chief Executive**, the president is the head of the executive branch of the government, and in charge of nominating judges, ambassadors, and other government officials.
- As **Commander in Chief**, the president is the leader of the Army, Navy, Air Force, and Marines.
- As **Foreign Policy Director**, the president guides U.S. relations with other nations.
- As **Legislative Leader**, the president proposes new laws to Congress.
- As **Chief of State**, the president presides over official ceremonies and is the leader of the American people.

Now that you know what all presidents have in common, let's find out what makes each one special....

GEORGE WASHINGTON President from 1789–1797

George Washington was so popular, many people wanted to crown him *king*! But George would have no part of it. Instead, he was elected president—the very first!

Martha Washington
What should people call the *first* first lady? "Lady Washington," "Mrs. President," or "Presidentress"? Down-to-earth Martha preferred plain old "Mrs. Washington."

Washington was the only president who never lived in the White House.

1732 - 1799

We cannot tell a lie—the Father of Our Country never did chop down a cherry tree.The story was started after his death.

North Carolina, *Vermont*, *Kentucky*, and *Tennessee* became states.

Washington had just one real tooth when he became president. His false teeth were made from cow's teeth and hippo bone.

In 1793, Washington put down the cornerstone for the U.S. Capitol.

1789 **1790** **1791** **1792** **1793** **1794** **1795** **1796** **1797**

- 1789: Washington is sworn in
- 1790: First American ship sails around the world
- 1791: Washington chooses site of the new nation's capital
- 1792: Construction begins on the White House; Washington is reelected
- 1794: First hotel in the U.S. opens
- 1796: John Adams defeats Thomas Jefferson in presidential election

Find the Washington stickers on sticker page A.

2 JOHN ADAMS

President from 1797–1801

Like Washington, Adams didn't have many teeth left when he became president, but he refused to wear dentures and so spoke with a lisp. Adams was the first president who had a son who became president, too.

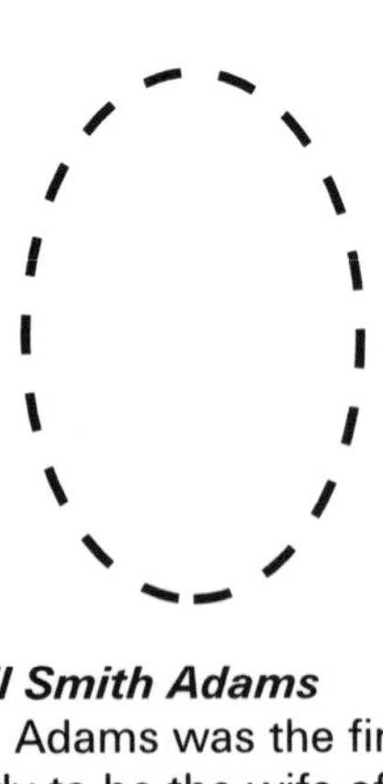

Abigail Smith Adams
Abigail Adams was the first first lady to be the wife of one president and mother of another—John Quincy Adams. She was also an early supporter of women's rights.

Adams and Jefferson were the only two signers of the Declaration of Independence to become president—and both died on the fiftieth anniversary of its signing!

1735 - 1826

In 1800, Adams started the Library of Congress.

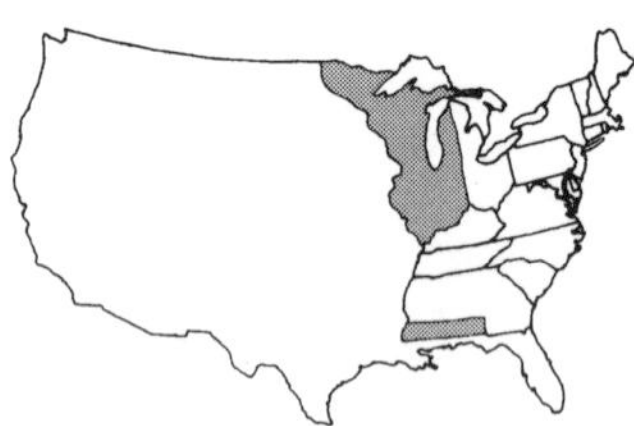

Mississippi and *Indiana* became territories.

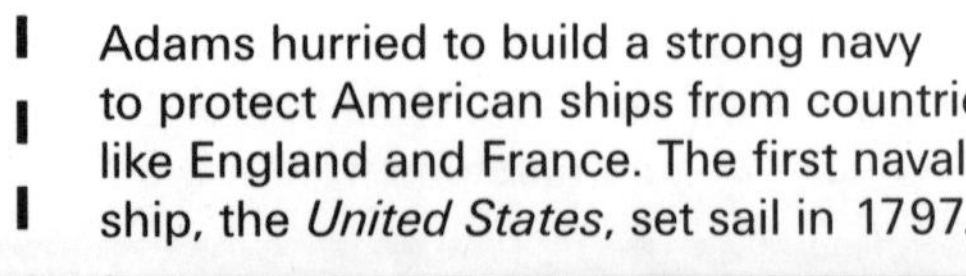

Adams hurried to build a strong navy to protect American ships from countries like England and France. The first naval ship, the *United States*, set sail in 1797.

In November 1800, Adams and his family moved into the brand-new White House—or at least into the six rooms that were finished.

1797 — World's first parachute jump is made in France from a balloon

1798 — Department of the Navy is created

1799

1800 — Washington D.C. officially becomes the nation's capital

Find the J. Adams stickers on sticker page A.

THOMAS JEFFERSON

President from 1801–1809

Thomas Jefferson never really thought of himself as a politician—but as a good citizen who wanted a country governed by the people. He was most proud of writing the Declaration of Independence and of starting the University of Virginia.

Martha "Patsy" Jefferson Randolph
Since Jefferson was a widower, his oldest daughter, Patsy, filled in as White House hostess. Her son was the first baby born in the White House.

A true believer in democracy, Jefferson had his dinner parties at a round table, and began the custom of shaking hands instead of bowing.

1743 - 1826

In 1806, explorers Lewis and Clark returned from their trip across the country with many gifts for the president—including a grizzly bear, which Jefferson kept in a cage on the White House lawn.

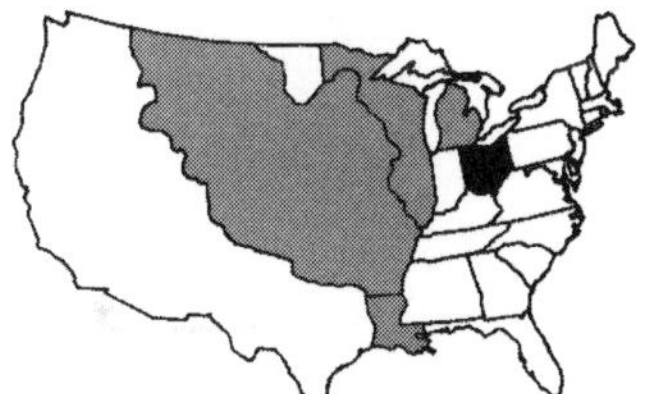

Ohio became a state. *Louisiana*, *Michigan*, and *Illinois* became territories.

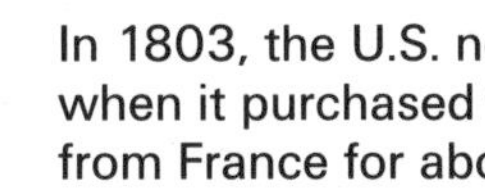

In 1803, the U.S. nearly doubled its size when it purchased the Louisiana Territory from France for about three cents an acre.

Jefferson was a great inventor, and was also one of the first Americans to make macaroni and grow tomatoes (which many people thought were poisonous).

1801	1802	1803	1804	1805	1806	1807	1808	1809
			First bananas are brought into the U.S. Jefferson is reelected	Explorers Lewis and Clark reach the Pacific Ocean		First passenger steamship	Jefferson outlaws the African slave trade	

Find the Jefferson stickers on sticker page A.

JAMES MADISON

President from 1809–1817

Known as “the Father of the Constitution,” James Madison helped write the Constitution and the Bill of Rights. But his good friend Thomas Jefferson had another nickname for the 5’4”, 100-pound president—“the Great Little Madison.”

Dolley Madison
Dolley Madison was preparing for a dinner party when the British invaded Washington. She fled with the Declaration of Independence and a portrait of George Washington. But the meal didn’t go to waste—the British soldiers ate it!

Madison was the first president to serve ice cream at the White House!

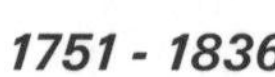

1751 - 1836

Madison was the first president to wear long pants instead of knee breeches and stockings.

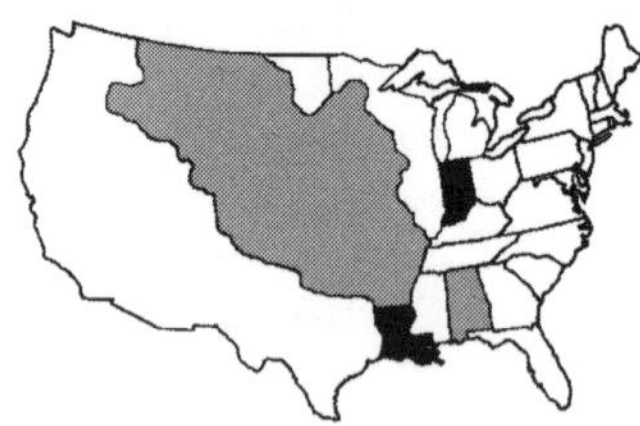

Louisiana and *Indiana* became states. *Missouri* and *Alabama* became territories.

During the War of 1812, the British set the White House and the Capitol on fire. Luckily, a summer thunderstorm put the fires out.

In 1814, Francis Scott Key wrote “The Star-Spangled Banner” as he watched the British bomb Fort McHenry.

1809 1810 1811 1812 1813 1814 1815 1816

- 1811: First national road is built
- 1812: War of 1812 begins; Madison is reelected
- 1814: War of 1812 ends
- 1815: First covered wagons take pioneers west

Find the Madison stickers on sticker page A.

JAMES MONROE

President from 1817–1825

James Monroe's time as president was so popular, it was known as "the Era of Good Feelings." Monroe didn't even have to campaign for reelection. He is best remembered for his foreign policy; the Monroe Doctrine told European countries to stay out of North and South America.

Elizabeth Kortright Monroe
Elegant Elizabeth Monroe was called *la belle américaine*, or the beautiful American, by the French when Monroe was minister there.

1758 - 1831

Monroe was the first president to ride in a steamboat.

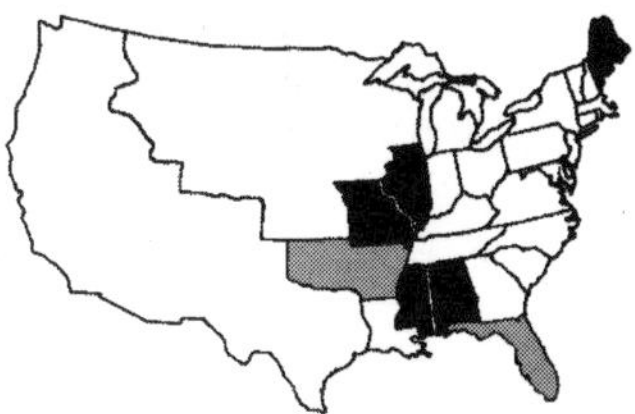

Mississippi, Illinois, Alabama, Maine, and *Missouri* became states. *Arkansas* and *Florida* became territories.

President Monroe started his term with a four-month trip around the U.S.A.—while he waited for the White House to be repaired.

In 1818, the first tin can in the U.S. was made.

In 1821, Troy Female Seminary, the first college for women in the U.S., opened.

1817	1818	1819	1820	1821	1822	1823	1824	1825
Monroe moves into the restored White House		The U.S. buys Florida from Spain	Monroe is reelected	First public high school in the U.S. opens				

Find the Monroe stickers on sticker page A.

JOHN QUINCY ADAMS

President from 1825–1829

A great speaker and deal maker, John Quincy Adams was nick-named "Old Man Eloquent"—but in private he was pretty cold and grim. Adams stayed in politics even after he was president, serving in Congress until the day he died.

Louisa Johnson Adams
Louisa Adams was the only first lady born outside the U.S. She was born and raised in England.

Adams got his daily workout by skinny-dipping in the Potomac River every morning.

No new states were admitted.

John Quincy Adams was the first president to have his photograph taken.

1767 - 1848

In 1827, the first ballet in the U.S. was performed.

In 1828, Noah Webster published the first American dictionary.

1825 — Erie Canal opens

1826 — First photograph

1827

1828 — First Native American newspaper

Find the J.Q. Adams stickers on sticker page A.

ANDREW JACKSON

President from 1829–1837

Andrew Jackson was truly the first "People's President," and his campaign included picnics and barbecues all across the country. The War of 1812 had made Jackson a national hero—and earned the "tough-as-a-hickory-tree" general the nickname "Old Hickory."

Rachel Donelson Jackson
Andrew Jackson's beloved wife, Rachel, died right before he took office. She was buried in the same dress she'd bought for his inauguration.

Jackson was the first president born in a log cabin.

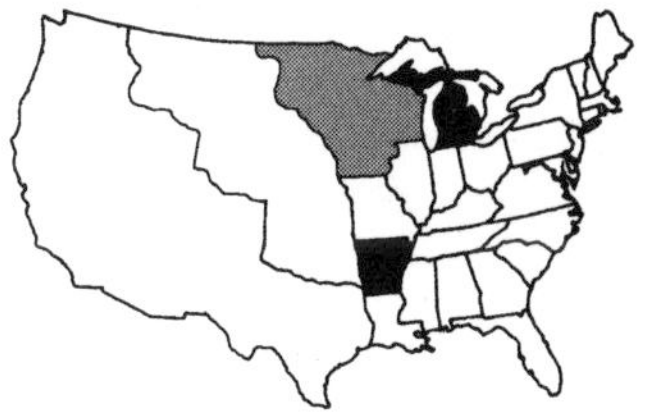

Arkansas and *Michigan* became states. *Wisconsin* became a territory.

Before he left the White House, Jackson had a huge open house party—complete with a 1,400-pound cheese. The smell of cheese stayed in the White House for weeks after he moved out.

1767 - 1845

In 1830, *Tom Thumb*, the first passenger steam locomotive in the U.S., was built—and Jackson became the first president to ride on a train.

In 1836, Texan fighters held off Mexican soldiers for two weeks at the famous battle of the Alamo.

1829 1830 1831 1832 1833 1834 1835 1836 1837

- 1829: First American encyclopedia
- 1830: Indian Removal Act gives the president the power to move eastern tribes west of the Mississippi
- 1832: First oranges and lemons are brought to the U.S.
- 1832: Andrew Jackson is reelected
- 1833: First public library in the U.S.
- 1833: First daily newspaper in the U.S.
- 1835: Assassination attempt is made on Jackson's life (luckily, the gun does not fire)
- 1835: White House gets running water
- 1835: Texas Revolution begins

Find the Jackson stickers on sticker page A.

MARTIN VAN BUREN

President from 1837–1841

Martin Van Buren was the first president to be born a U.S. citizen. (Others had been born before the U.S. became a nation.) Although Van Buren wasn't born wealthy, he had a reputation for very expensive tastes.

Hannah Hoes Van Buren
Hannah, Van Buren's wife and childhood sweetheart, died nearly twenty years before he became president, and he never remarried.

Van Buren was nicknamed "Old Kinderhook" after the town where he was born—and some say it's where the expression "O.K." came from.

1782 - 1862

During Van Buren's term, thousands of banks and businesses closed, and millions of people lost everything they'd worked for.

Iowa became a territory.

In 1838, 14,000 Cherokee were forced to leave Georgia and march to Oklahoma. It became known as the Trail of Tears because so many people died along the way.

In 1839, the first baseball diamond was built in a cow pasture in Cooperstown, NY.

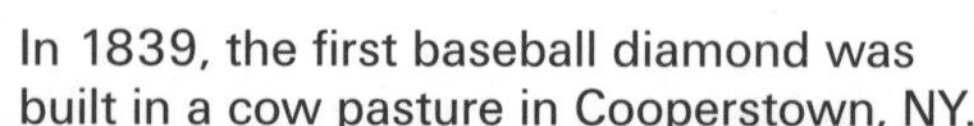

- 1837: First steel plow; Queen Victoria is crowned Queen of England
- 1838: White House gets hot water
- 1839: Charles Goodyear patents rubber-making process
- 1840: First photograph of the moon; Samuel Morse patents the telegraph

Find the Van Buren stickers on sticker page A.

WILLIAM HENRY HARRISON

President from March–April 1841

William Henry Harrison's presidency was the shortest in history. He caught a cold on the same day he was sworn in and died of pneumonia just one month later. Like Washington and Jackson, he had been a famous war hero.

Anna Symmes Harrison
Anna Harrison was still living in Ohio and preparing to move to Washington when Harrison died. She is the only first lady to be the wife of one president and the grand-mother of another—Benjamin Harrison.

To set himself apart from Van Buren and his fancy tastes, Harrison ran as "the Log Cabin Candidate"...even though he lived in a mansion.

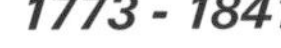

1773 - 1841

Harrison liked to get up early and do his own shopping.

No new states were admitted.

Harrison was born on the Virginia plantation where the first Thanksgiving meal was held—two years before the famous Pilgrim dinner.

In 1841, Harrison delivered the longest inaugural address ever. In fact, his two-hour speech (which he gave outside in the cold) might have cost him his life.

1841

Harrison is sworn in

Harrison becomes the first president to die in office

Find the W.H. Harrison stickers on sticker page A.

10 JOHN TYLER

President from 1841–1845

John Tyler was the first vice president to take over for a dead president. (And he hadn't even known President Harrison was sick!) Nicknaming him "His Accidency," Tyler's own party tried to take away much of his power. But Tyler refused...and soon became the first president without a political party.

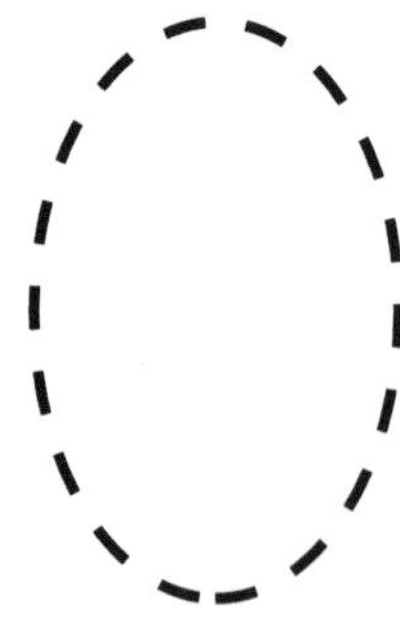

Julia Gardiner Tyler
Tyler's first wife, Letitia, died a year after moving to the White House. In 1844, Tyler married Julia Gardiner—who started the tradition of having "Hail to the Chief" played for the president.

Years after he was president, during the Civil War, Tyler seceded with the South and became a congressman for the Confederate States of America. Because of this, until 1915, Tyler was officially a traitor.

1790 - 1862

Tyler had the most children of any president—fifteen! Tyler and his family were also animal lovers and always had lots of pets around.

Florida became a state.

In 1843, the 2,000-mile-long Oregon Trail opened for pioneers moving west.

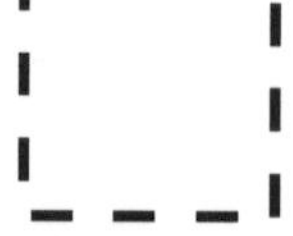

In 1844, Samuel Morse sent the first telegraph message: "What hath God wrought."

1841 **1842** **1843** **1844** **1845**

1842: First official baseball club; Letitia Tyler dies

1844: Tyler marries Julia Gardiner

Find the Tyler stickers on sticker page A.

11 JAMES KNOX POLK

President from 1845–1849

James Polk sailed into office on the wave of "Manifest Destiny." This was the popular belief that the U.S. was meant to expand across all of North America. Hardworking Polk increased the size of the U.S. more than any president since Jefferson.

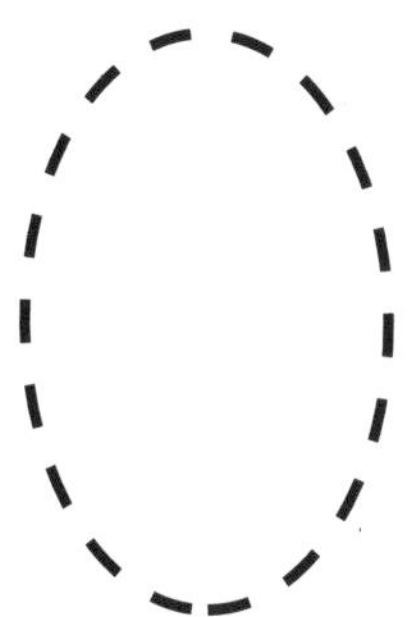

Sarah Childress Polk
Sarah Polk was one of the first first ladies to have a real say in her husband's work. She served as Polk's secretary and even helped him write speeches.

Polk was the first "dark horse"—or unexpected—candidate. He was so unknown that his opponent's slogan was "Who is Polk?"

1795 - 1849

James and Sarah Polk hosted the first formal Thanksgiving dinner ever served at the White House.

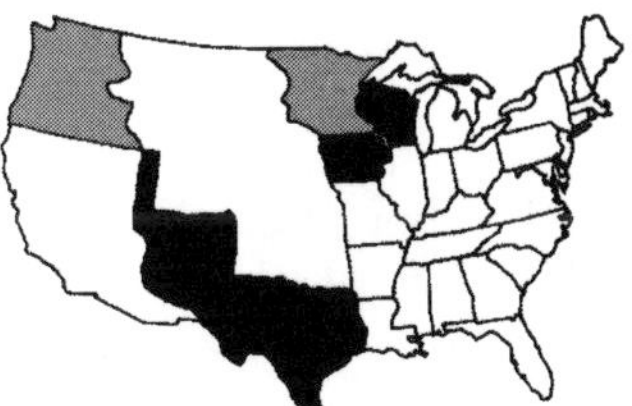

Texas, *Iowa*, and *Wisconsin* became states. *Oregon* and *Minnesota* became territories.

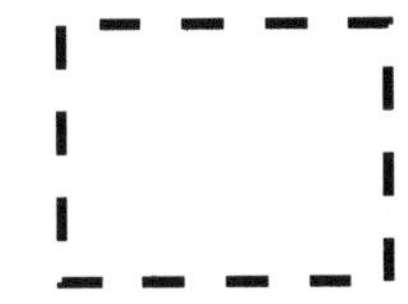

In 1847, the first U.S. postage stamps were made. Until then, people had just paid the postman.

In 1848, the first stick of chewing gum in the U.S. was sold.

1846 1847 1848 1849

Smithsonian Institution is founded

Mexican War begins

Gold is discovered in California

Mexican War ends

First women's rights convention is held in Seneca Falls, NY

Find the Polk stickers on sticker page A.

ZACHARY TAYLOR

President from 1849–1850

Small and rather sloppy, General "Old Rough and Ready" Taylor was a Mexican War hero—not a politician. He'd never even voted in a presidential election!

Mary Elizabeth "Betty" Taylor Bliss
Because her mother, Margaret, did not want to be first lady, Taylor's daughter Betty served as White House hostess in her place. Mrs. Taylor chose to stay in her room and refused to pose for pictures.

By the time Taylor became president, the Underground Railroad was already helping thousands of slaves escape. Harriet Tubman was one of its leaders.

1784 - 1850

Taylor brought his faithful warhorse, Old Whitey, to Washington with him and let him graze on the White House lawn—until sightseers started plucking Whitey's tail hairs!

No new states were admitted.

In 1849, the California Gold Rush began with 80,000 prospectors racing west.

In 1850, Taylor took part in a hot Fourth of July ceremony at the unfinished Washington Monument, then went home to have some milk and cherries. Five days later, he died from a "digestive illness."

1849
- Safety pin is invented
- Harriet Tubman escapes from slavery

1850
- Taylor dies

Find the Taylor stickers on sticker page A.

MILLARD FILLMORE

President from 1850–1853

The biggest question of Millard Fillmore's day was whether new states should allow slavery or not. The Northern states wanted to end it. The Southern ones wanted to keep it—and threatened to break away if they didn't get their way. Fillmore tried to compromise—it was called the Compromise of 1850.

Abigail Powers Fillmore
Twenty-one-year-old Abigail met nineteen-year-old Millard when he was her student in a one-room schoolhouse. Abigail was the first first lady to continue working after she was married.

Thanks to the Fillmores, the White House got many modern conveniences, including its first stove and tub.

1800 - 1874

Mrs. Fillmore was so shocked to find the White House had no library, she asked the president to have Congress pay for one and picked out the books herself.

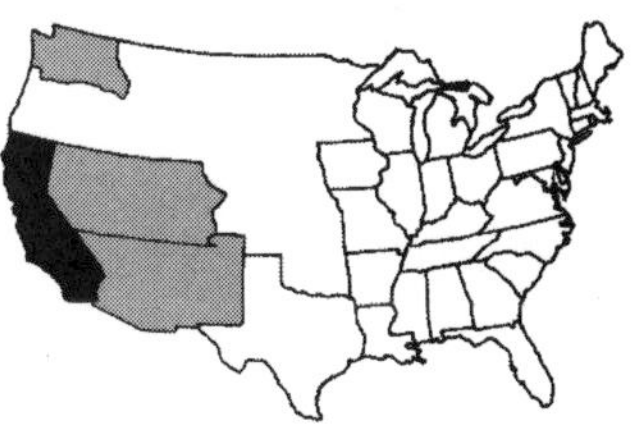

California became a state. *New Mexico*, *Utah*, and *Washington* became territories.

In 1851, Amelia Bloomer shocked people by wearing lace pants under a short skirt—a style that was soon called "bloomers."

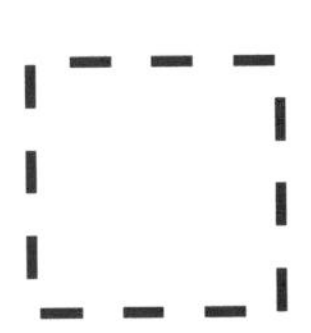

In 1852, Harriet Beecher Stowe published her antislavery novel, *Uncle Tom's Cabin*.

1850 — Compromise of 1850 outlaws slavery in CA, but allows Southern slave owners to capture slaves who escape North

1851 — Isaac Singer patents his sewing machine

1852 — First successful airship is flown

1853

Find the Fillmore stickers on sticker page B.

FRANKLIN PIERCE

President from 1853–1857

Handsome Franklin Pierce never, ever lost an election. He hoped to calm down the North and South by letting new states decide for themselves whether to allow slavery, but this only started more fighting for control.

Jane Appleton Pierce
For two years after her eleven-year-old son was killed in a train accident, Jane Pierce refused to appear in public. He was, in fact, their third son to die.

Another "dark horse" candidate, Pierce ran on the slogan "We *Polked* you in 1844. We'll *Pierce* you in 1852."

1804 - 1869

Pierce was known to race his horse and carriage through the streets of Washington—and was once even arrested for knocking over an old woman.

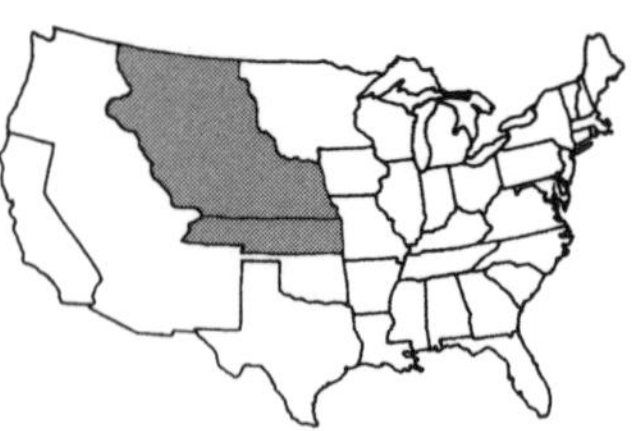

Kansas and *Nebraska* became territories.

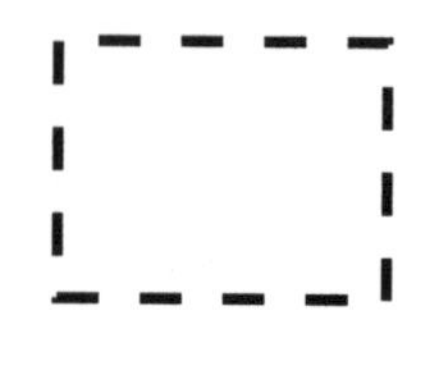

In 1854, the first U.S. oil company—Pennsylvania Rock Oil—was formed.

In 1856, the first U.S. kindergarten opened.

1853 **1854** **1855** **1856**

The U.S. buys parts of Arizona and New Mexico from Mexico

Kansas-Nebraska Act is passed, allowing states to choose whether to allow slavery

Republican Party is formed

Find the Pierce stickers on sticker page B.

15 JAMES BUCHANAN

President from 1857-1861

James Buchanan had the unusual problem of being nearsighted in one eye and farsighted in the other—but he still managed to have the neatest handwriting of any president.

Harriet Lane
Buchanan was the only president who never married. His niece, Harriet Lane, served as his White House hostess.

1791 - 1868

Buchanan was the first president to have a royal guest stay in the White House—England's Prince Albert. Buchanan even slept on the sofa so the prince could use his bed.

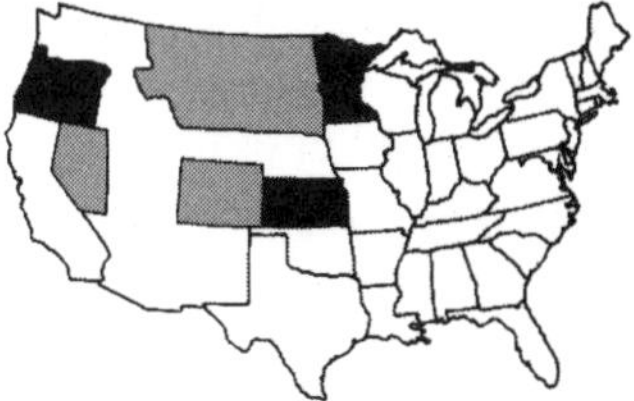

Minnesota, *Oregon*, and *Kansas* became states. *Colorado*, *Nevada*, and the *Dakotas* became territories.

Because Buchanan had been working in England, he was able to avoid the subject of slavery in his campaign—and easily beat the new Republican, antislavery party.

In 1860, Pony Express service began carrying mail across the West.

In 1861, seven Southern states broke away from the Union and formed the Confederate States of America.

1857 1858 1859 1860 1861

- First passenger elevator
- Panic of 1857 puts millions out of work
- Darwin publishes his theory of evolution
- South Carolina secedes from the Union

Find the Buchanan stickers on sticker page B.

ABRAHAM LINCOLN

President from 1861–1865

Abraham Lincoln was one of America's greatest leaders. If it weren't for him, we might be two separate nations today! Still, Lincoln never lost his knack for telling jokes and stories—or his pioneer accent. He was the first president born west of the original thirteen states.

Mary Todd Lincoln
Mary Lincoln's White House years were far from happy. Besides the great war, she had to face the deaths of her son Willie and her husband.

One month after Lincoln was sworn in, the new Confederate army began firing on Fort Sumter, officially beginning the Civil War.

In 1863, Lincoln issued the Emancipation Proclamation, freeing slaves in the Confederate States—but not in the Union.

1809 - 1865

Lincoln was the first president to wear a beard in office—which he grew at the suggestion of an eleven-year-old girl. He was also the first president to have his picture on a coin.

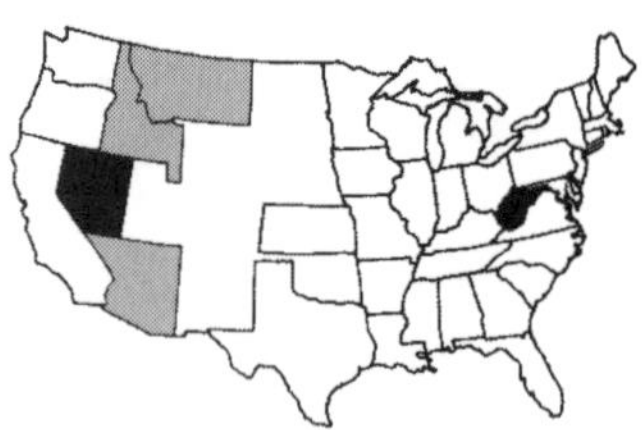

West Virginia and *Nevada* became states. *Arizona*, *Idaho*, and *Montana* became territories.

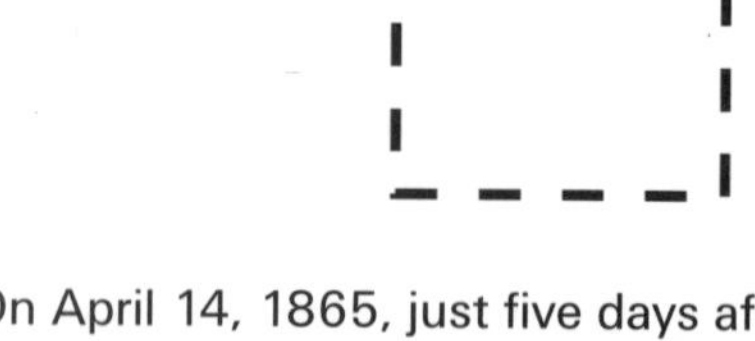

On April 14, 1865, just five days after the South surrendered, John Wilkes Booth snuck into the president's box at Ford's Theater and shot Lincoln in the back of the head.

1861
- Civil War begins
- U.S. issues its first paper money

1862
- Lincoln's son Willie dies

1863
- First roller skates
- Lincoln makes Thanksgiving a national holiday

1864
- Lincoln is reelected

1865
- General Robert E. Lee surrenders and the Civil War ends
- Lincoln is assassinated

Find the Lincoln stickers on sticker page B.

ANDREW JOHNSON

President from 1865–1869

Andrew Johnson never went to school and had to teach himself to read. Like Lincoln, he wanted to bring the North and South back together. Many congressmen did not agree with this approach and tried unsuccessfully to remove Johnson from office through an impeachment trial.

Eliza McCardle Johnson
Married when she was just sixteen, Eliza Johnson taught her young husband writing and math.

1808 - 1875

Johnson was trained as a tailor and opened his own shop when he was just seventeen. As president, he sometimes still sewed his own clothes.

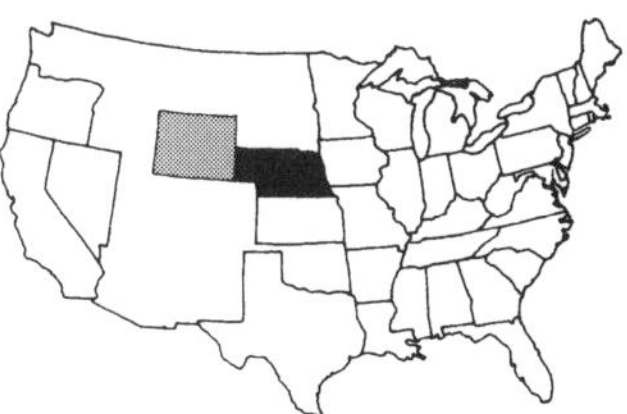

Nebraska became a state.
Wyoming became a territory.

In 1866, the first U.S. Civil Rights Act was passed. The Act gave Americans of every race equal rights under the law.

In 1866, Alfred Nobel of Sweden invented dynamite.

In 1867, Secretary of State William Seward bought Alaska from Russia for about 2 cents an acre. Critics called it "Seward's Folly"—until gold was found there. Then it was called the biggest bargain in history.

1865
First train robbery
13th Amendment outlaws slavery

1866
Civil Rights Act of 1866 is passed
American Society for the Prevention of Cruelty to Animals (ASPCA) is founded

1867
First typewriter

1868
House impeaches Johnson, but the Senate acquits him
14th Amendment makes former slaves citizens and gives them full civil rights

1869

Find the A. Johnson stickers on sticker page B.

ULYSSES S. GRANT

President from 1869-1877

As the general who led the Union armies to victory, Ulysses S. Grant was a presidential shoo-in. Grant was actually born Hiram Ulysses Grant. But when his name was put down as Ulysses Simpson Grant by mistake on his West Point application, Grant liked the initials U.S.G. so much better than H.U.G., he decided to keep them.

Julia Dent Grant
Julia Grant's White House years were the happiest of her life—and if it had been up to "Mrs. G.," as Grant called her, he would have run for a third term.

"Let Us Have Peace" became the theme of Grant's campaign—and is even engraved on his tomb in New York City.

1822 - 1885

As president, Grant once was given a speeding ticket for riding too fast through the streets of Washington.

Colorado became a state.

In 1869, the first cross-country railroad in the U.S. was completed and marked by a golden spike.

In 1872, Grant named the first national park—Yellowstone, home of Old Faithful.

1869 — Susan B. Anthony and Elizabeth Cady Stanton form the National Woman Suffrage Association

1870 — Brooklyn Bridge is begun

1871 — P.T. Barnum opens "the Greatest Show on Earth"; Great Chicago fire destroys much of the city

1872 — Victoria Woodhull becomes the first woman to run for president; Grant is reelected

1873

1874 — First zoo in the U.S.

1875

1876 — Alexander Graham Bell invents the telephone; Sioux and Cheyenne warriors defeat Gen. Custer at the battle of Little Bighorn

Find the Grant stickers on sticker page B.

RUTHERFORD B. HAYES

President from 1877–1881

Rutherford Birchard Hayes was an honest, religious man, who began his days with a prayer and ended them with a hymn. Still, his election was the most disputed ever. It took Congress months to decide which candidate had the most electoral votes. In the end, Hayes won by only one, and was called by many "His Fraudulency."

Lucy Webb Hayes
Lucy Hayes was the first first lady with a college degree, and the first to be called "first lady." She was also known as "Lemonade Lucy" because she never served alcohol in the White House.

In 1877, Thomas Edison went to the White House to show his new phonograph to the president.

1822 - 1893

Hayes was the first president to have a telephone and a typewriter in the White House.

No new states were admitted.

In 1878, the Hayeses hosted the first official Easter Egg Roll on the White House lawn—which is still held every year.

In 1880, the first hot dog was served in St. Louis, Missouri.

1877	1878	1879	1880	1881

- 1877: Reconstruction ends
- 1879: Thomas Edison invents the light bulb
- 1880: Hayes becomes the first president to visit the west coast
- 1880: Metropolitan Museum of Art opens in New York City

Find the Hayes stickers on sticker page B.

20 JAMES A. GARFIELD

President from March–Sept. 1881

Four months after he was sworn in, James Abram Garfield was shot as he walked through a train station. He died from blood poisoning ten weeks later. The killer had hoped to get a job from the new president, and was angry because he never did.

Lucretia Rudolph Garfield
Lucretia "Crete" Garfield was recovering from an illness at the New Jersey shore when she heard that her husband had been shot, but she returned to Washington right away and helped nurse him until he died.

Garfield did most of his campaigning from his front porch in Ohio—where people came by train to hear him speak.

1831 - 1881

Garfield was the first left-handed president. He liked to show off by writing Greek with one hand and Latin with the other—at the same time!

No new states were admitted.

In 1881, the first malted milk was served. Yum!

Also in 1881, nurse Clara Barton founded the American Red Cross.

1881

- First summer camp in the U.S.
- Garfield is shot by Charles Guiteau
- Garfield dies

Find the Garfield stickers on sticker page B.

CHESTER A. ARTHUR

President from 1881–1885

Tall, handsome Chester Alan Arthur liked fancy clothes so much, he had eighty pairs of pants! He liked fine furniture, too, and had the White House redecorated from top to bottom in the latest fashion.

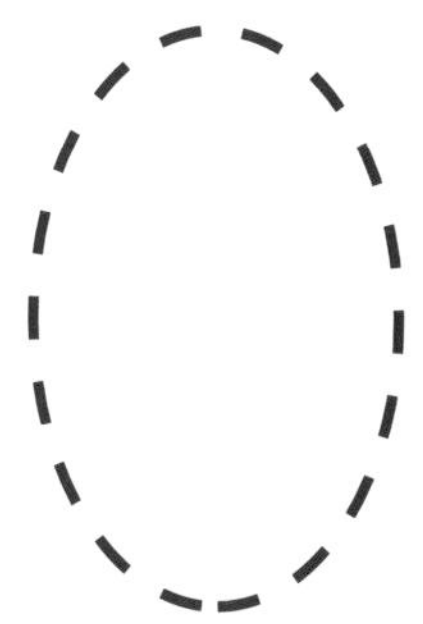

Ellen Herndon Arthur
Ellen "Nell" Arthur died just a year before her husband became president. From then on, Arthur placed flowers by her picture every day.

Arthur shook so many hands when he campaigned, his hand swelled up and his ring had to be filed off.

1829 - 1886

Arthur liked to stay up very late, and hardly ever went to bed before two a.m. One of his favorite things to do was give guests tours of Washington in the middle of the night.

No new states were admitted.

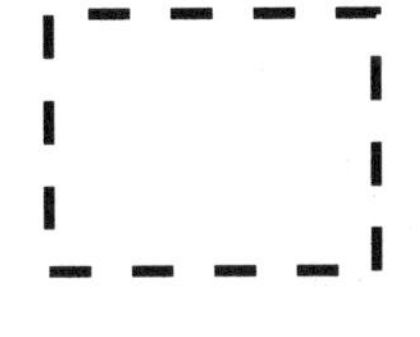

In 1885, the world's first skyscraper was built—the ten-story Home Insurance Building in Chicago.

In 1883, Buffalo Bill Cody put on his first Wild West Show.

1881 — Shoot-out at the O.K. Corral

1882

1883 — Brooklyn Bridge opens

1884

1885 — Washington Monument is dedicated

Find the Arthur stickers on sticker page B.

GROVER CLEVELAND

President from 1885–1889

Grover Cleveland was actually born Stephen Grover Cleveland, but he dropped his first name when he was a young man. Cleveland was so large and jolly, his nieces and nephews called him Uncle Jumbo.

Cleveland was the only president to get married in the White House.

Frances Folsom Cleveland
Twenty-one-year-old Frances Cleveland was the youngest first lady ever—and one of the most popular.

No new states were admitted.

A "do-it-yourself" kind of president, Cleveland even went without a secretary for a while and answered the White House phone himself.

1837-1908

Also in 1886, Cleveland dedicated the Statue of Liberty in New York City.

In 1886, John Pemberton invented Coca-Cola as a health tonic.

1885 **1886** **1887** **1888** **1889**

1886: Cleveland marries Frances Folsom

1888: Kodak box camera is introduced; National Geographic Society is founded

Find the Cleveland stickers on sticker page B.

BENJAMIN HARRISON

President from 1889-1893

The grandson of President William Henry Harrison, Benjamin Harrison was the last president to wear a beard, and was so stiff and formal, people often called him "the human iceberg."

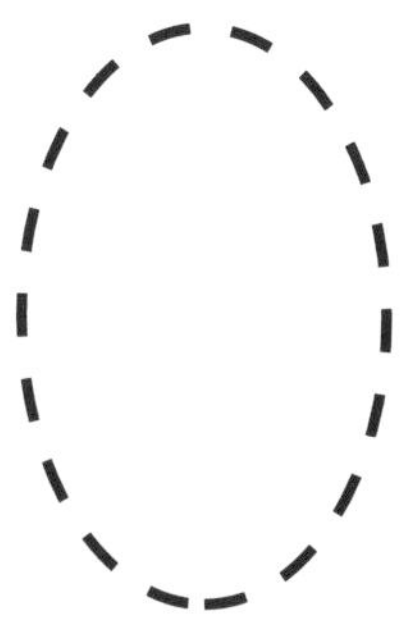

Caroline Scott Harrison
Caroline Harrison put up the first White House Christmas tree. Sadly, she died in the White House just two weeks before the 1892 election.

1833 - 1901

Harrison was the first president to have electricity in the White House—but his wife and he were so afraid to touch the switches, they left the lights on all night long.

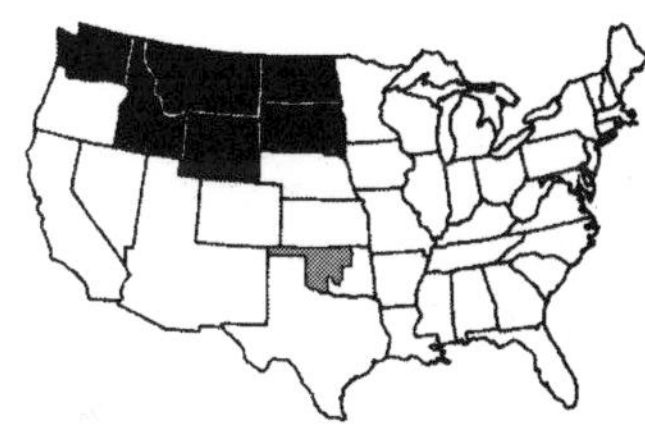

North Dakota, South Dakota, Montana, Washington, Idaho, and *Wyoming* became states. *Oklahoma* became a territory.

Nicknamed "Little Ben" because he was just 5′6″ tall, Harrison told voters not to worry—"Grandfather's Hat Fits."

In 1891, basketball was invented by a gym teacher named James Naismith.

In 1892, Ellis Island opened to receive new immigrants pouring into New York.

1889 1890 1891 1892 1893

- 1889: White settlers claim 2 million acres of former Indian land in Oklahoma in one day
- First movie camera
- 1890: Sitting Bull is killed
- 1892: Caroline Harrison dies
- First gas-powered car in the U.S.

Find the B. Harrison stickers on sticker page B.

GROVER CLEVELAND

President from 1893–1897

Grover Cleveland was the only president to be reelected after being voted out of office. And his second daughter, Esther, was the first child of a president to be born in the White House.

Frances Folsom Cleveland
At the end of Cleveland's first term, Frances Cleveland had told the White House servants she wanted "everything just the way it is now when we come back." Obviously, she knew what she was saying!

In 1893, Cleveland had a tumor secretly removed from his mouth—and the operation stayed a secret until years after his death.

In 1893, the world's biggest Ferris wheel (it was 25 stories tall!) was built for the Chicago World's Columbian Exposition.

1837 - 1908

The Baby Ruth candy bar was named after Cleveland's baby daughter Ruth.

Utah became a state.

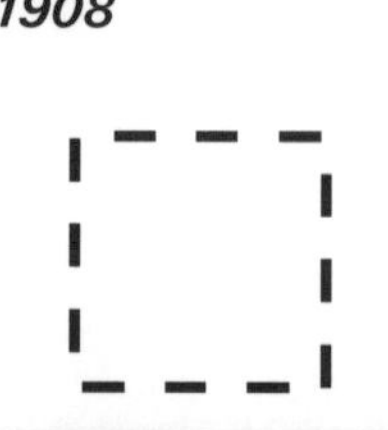

In 1896, the first modern Olympic Games were held in Athens, Greece.

1893
- Panic of 1893 starts economic depression
- First zipper
- Canada introduces ice hockey to the U.S.

1894
- Cleveland makes Labor Day a national holiday

1895
- Dr. John Harvey Kellogg invents cornflakes
- First professional football game
- First radio

1896
- First comic strip
- Henry Ford builds his first car

1897
- First campaign buttons

Find the Cleveland stickers on sticker page B.

WILLIAM McKINLEY

President from 1897–1901

It was during William McKinley's term that the U.S. became a true "world power." The Spanish-American War was won in just 100 days—then the U.S. acquired Puerto Rico, the Philippines, Guam, and Hawaii.

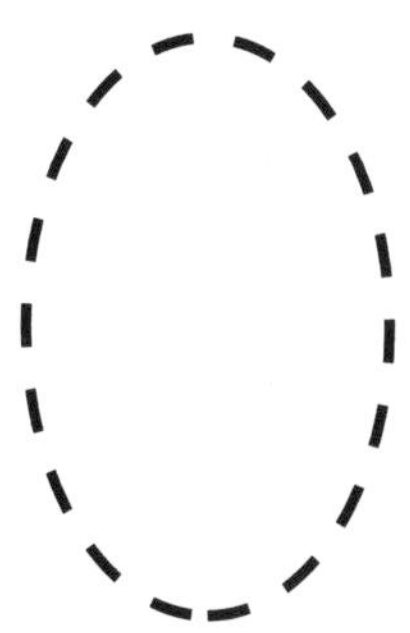

Ida Saxton McKinley
President McKinley was completely devoted to his wife, Ida–who suffered from what people then called "the falling sickness." Today we call it epilepsy.

McKinley never campaigned without a lucky red carnation in his buttonhole. His home state, Ohio, later made it their state flower.

1843 - 1901

After the sinking of the battleship *Maine* in 1898, "Remember the *Maine*!" became the battle cry of the Spanish-American War.

McKinley was the first president to ride to his inauguration in a car–and the only one to have a parrot who could whistle "Yankee Doodle."

Hawaii became a territory.

McKinley was assassinated just six months into his second term. After that, Congress gave the Secret Service the job of protecting the president full-time.

1897 — First U.S. subway opens in Boston

1898 — Spanish-American War

1899

1900 — McKinley is reelected

1901 — Oil is discovered in Texas; McKinley is shot by anarchist Leon Czolgosz as he shakes hands in a receiving line; he dies eight days later

Find the McKinley stickers on sticker page C.

THEODORE ROOSEVELT

President from 1901–1909

Theodore Roosevelt was the youngest president, taking over for McKinley when he was only 42. Roosevelt worked to make the U.S. stronger abroad and at home, where he believed every American deserved a "square deal"—fair wages, fair prices, and safe, healthy conditions.

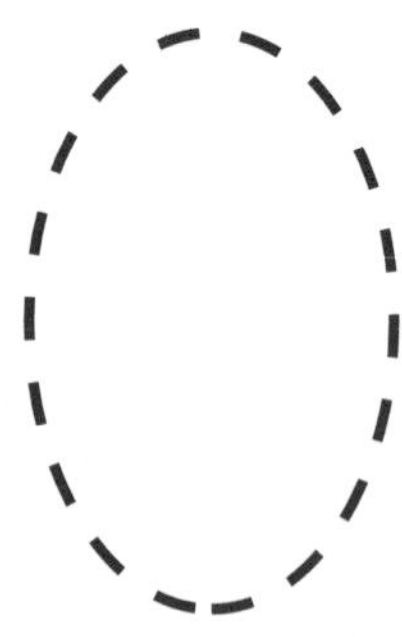

Edith Carow Roosevelt
Edith Roosevelt grew up next door to the future president (and her future husband). They were playmates, but they did not get married until after the death of Roosevelt's first wife.

Teddy Roosevelt was a sickly boy, but he grew up to be one of our most athletic presidents. He liked to hunt, climb mountains, and practice boxing and judo.

1858 - 1919

Roosevelt was the first president to ride in an airplane and a submarine.

Oklahoma became a state.

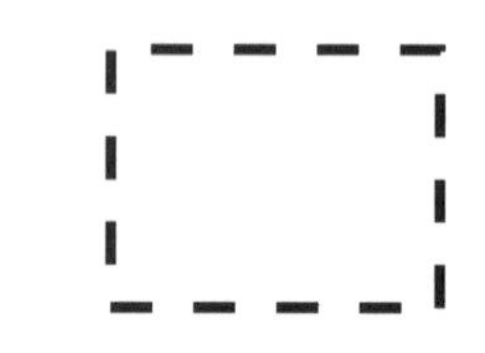

In 1902, a toymaker saw a cartoon showing T.R. on a hunting trip saying "No" to shooting a little bear cub. The toymaker named one of his stuffed bears "Teddy's bear" and put it in the window—and the teddy bear was born!

Nicknamed "the Great Conservationist," Roosevelt established hundreds of national forests and parks.

1901 1902 1903 1904 1905 1906 1907 1908

- First World Series
- Wright brothers' first airplane flight (1903)
- First reported UFO sighting
- Work begins on the Panama Canal
- First ice-cream cone and first hamburger (1904)
- Roosevelt is reelected
- Einstein publishes his theory of relativity (1905)
- Roosevelt is the first president to win the Nobel Peace Prize (1906)
- Great San Francisco earthquake and fire
- First radio broadcast
- Ford's Model T goes on sale (1908)
- First Mother's Day celebration

Find the T. Roosevelt stickers on sticker page C.

WILLIAM H. TAFT

President from 1909–1913

William Howard Taft loved the law—but he did not love being president. His favorite job came later, when President Harding made him Chief Justice of the Supreme Court. Taft is the only man to have done both jobs.

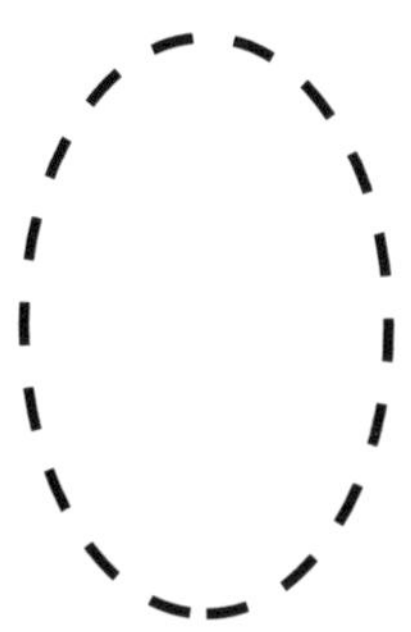

Helen "Nellie" Taft
Before she even moved into the White House, Nellie Taft ordered the first presidential automobiles and had the old White House stables turned into a garage.

1857 - 1930

"Big Bill" Taft was the biggest president—so big he once got stuck in the White House tub. After that, he had a new tub put in—big enough to hold four men!

Arizona and *New Mexico* became states. *Alaska* became a territory.

Before he left office, Theodore Roosevelt hand-picked Taft to be his successor. The public soon nicknamed him Bill—but his good friends called him Will.

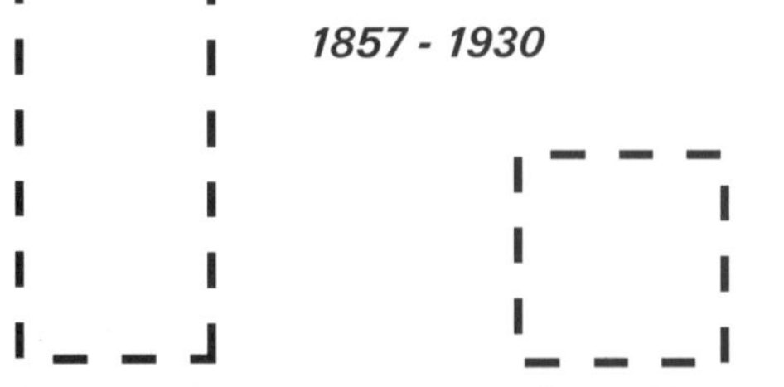

Taft was a big baseball fan, and was the first president to throw out the first ball on opening day.

In 1911, the first comic book was published.

1909 **1910** **1911** **1912** **1913**

- First cartoon
- National Association for the Advancement of Colored People (NAACP) is founded
- North Pole is discovered
- Boy Scouts of America is founded
- First Father's Day
- Oreo cookie is invented
- South Pole is discovered
- First Indianapolis 500 car race
- Girl Scouts of the U.S.A. is founded
- The *Titanic* sinks

Find the Taft stickers on sticker page C.

WOODROW WILSON

President from 1913–1921

Woodrow Wilson was one of the most scholarly presidents, earning over a dozen degrees. He led the U.S. to victory in World War I, but more than anything he wanted world peace. Wilson's idea for a "League of Nations" led to the formation of today's United Nations.

Edith Bolling Wilson
It's said that Edith Wilson was directly descended from Pocahontas. She married the president in 1915, one year after his first wife died. After Wilson had a stroke in 1919, she helped him with many of his presidential duties.

At first, Wilson promised to keep the U.S. out of WWI. But by 1917, it was clear that in order to make the world "safe for democracy," the U.S. would have to join in.

World War I ended in 1918, after four long years and the loss of 10 million soldiers. It was supposed to be "the war to end all wars."

1856 - 1924

During WWI, Wilson kept sheep on the White House lawn. Their wool was used to make army blankets—and the lawn never had to be mowed.

Puerto Rico became a territory.

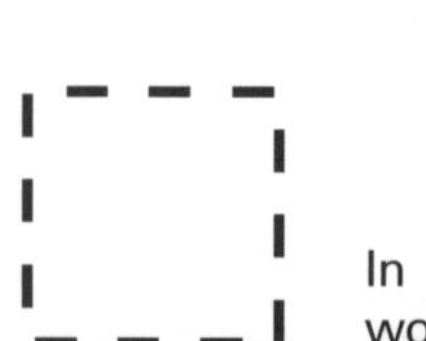

In 1920, the 14th Amendment gave women the right to vote.

1913

1914
- Panama Canal opens
- World War I begins

1915
- First U.S. taxicabs

1916
- Wilson is reelected

1917
- Russian Revolution
- U.S. joins in WWI
- Prohibition outlaws liquor

1918
- First airmail delivery
- World War I ends

1919
- Wilson's stroke

1920
- League of Nations is formed—but Congress votes not to join
- Wilson receives Nobel Peace Prize

Find the Wilson stickers on sticker page C.

WARREN G. HARDING

President from 1921–1923

Warren Gamaliel Harding loved poker—and even lost President Benjamin Harrison's White House china in a game! There were many scandals in Harding's administration—but they were not exposed until after his sudden death on a goodwill trip across the country.

Florence Kling Harding
"The Duchess," as President Harding called his wife, Florence, liked to edit her husband's speeches. She also liked to lead White House tours.

Harding promised the country a "return to normalcy" after World War I. He was the first president that women could vote for.

1865 - 1923

Every day, Harding's dog Laddie Boy would bring him the morning paper. After the president died, paperboys around the country collected pennies to build a statue of Laddie Boy—which is now on display at the Smithsonian Institution.

No new states were admitted.

In 1921, the first Miss America pageant was held.

In 1922, Harding gave the first presidential speech over the radio.

1921
- First Band-Aids

1922
- Lincoln Memorial is dedicated
- Soviet Union is formed
- First water skis

1923
- Harding dies suddenly of a mysterious illness (doctors believe it was a heart attack)

Find the Harding stickers on sticker page C.

CALVIN COOLIDGE

President from 1923–1929

"Silent Cal" Coolidge was a man of few words and few smiles—but he governed during the oh-so-carefree "Roaring Twenties." When President Harding died, V.P. Coolidge was visiting his family in Vermont. So his father, a justice of the peace, got to swear in Coolidge in the very house where he was born.

Grace Goodhue Coolidge
Grace Coolidge was just about the most popular American woman of her day. Before she was married, she taught lipreading to the deaf, and as first lady once gave a speech entirely in sign language.

Coolidge believed the less government the better, and in many ways let the country run itself. Coolidge also got more sleep than any other president—around eleven hours a day.

1872 - 1933

Coolidge got his exercise riding a mechanical horse he had installed in his White House bedroom.

No new states were admitted.

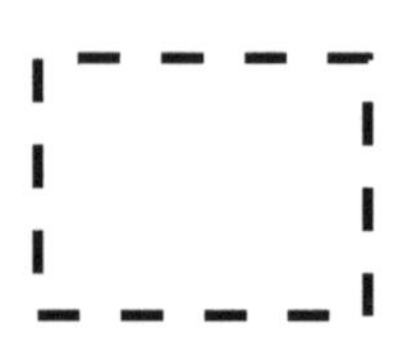

In 1927, Charles Lindbergh made the first nonstop solo flight across the Atlantic.

The Coolidges loved animals and got all kinds of pets as gifts, but their favorite was a raccoon they named Rebecca—who had actually been given to them as an exotic Thanksgiving main dish!

1923

1924
- Native Americans are made "official" U.S. citizens
- Coolidge wins election

1925
- John Scopes is convicted for teaching evolution in school

1926
- First rocket flight
- First talking movie

1927
- Babe Ruth sets home run record
- First TV

1928
- Mickey Mouse debuts

1929
- First vending machine

Find the Coolidge stickers on sticker page C.

HERBERT HOOVER

President from 1929–1933

Until Herbert Clark Hoover (or "Bert," as his friends called him) ran for president, he had never run for office. He was a self-made millionaire devoted to helping people. But he also led the U.S. through one of its worst economic times.

Lou Henry Hoover
Lou and Herbert Hoover met at Stanford University, where she was the first woman to get a geology degree. She and Hoover spoke several languages, including Chinese, which they used when they didn't want others to know what they were saying.

Hoover's campaign promise to put "a chicken in every pot—and a car in every garage" was one which he couldn't keep.

1874 - 1964

During the Great Depression, Hoover's name became a dirty word. Shantytowns were called "Hoovervilles." Newspapers were "Hoover blankets." And the wild rabbits and squirrels people killed for food were called "Hoover hogs."

No new states were admitted.

In 1929, the same year Hoover took office, the stock market crashed, and the Great Depression began.

In 1931, the Empire State Building was opened—and was the tallest buiding in the world for nearly forty years.

1929 — First Academy Awards

1930 — First pinball machine

1931 — "The Star-Spangled Banner" becomes the national anthem; First air conditioner

1932 — Amelia Earhart flies solo across the Atlantic

1933

Find the Hoover stickers on sticker page C.

32 FRANKLIN D. ROOSEVELT

President from 1933-1945

Franklin Delano Roosevelt led the U.S. out of the Great Depression and to victory in World War II. And he did it all from a wheelchair—since polio had left him paralyzed at the age of 39.

Anna Eleanor Roosevelt
Little did Eleanor Roosevelt know when her uncle, President Teddy Roosevelt, gave her away that she was marrying a future president too. After FDR lost use of his legs, she traveled around the world as his eyes and ears.

FDR was elected four times—more than any other president. Later, in 1951, Congress passed the 22nd Amendment, limiting the president to just two terms.

1882 - 1945

FDR's Scottie, Fala, got the nickname "the Informer" from the Secret Service—who knew that whenever they saw Fala, the president couldn't be far away.

No new states were admitted.

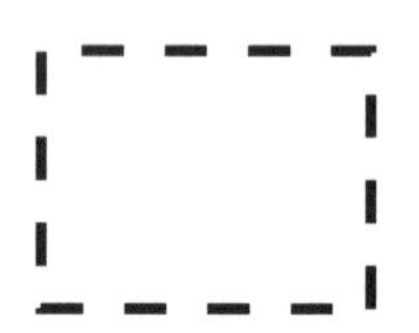

FDR had hoped to keep the U.S. out of WWII. But by 1941, he knew the U.S. had to join in too. Sadly, he died just months before Germany and Japan surrendered.

In 1933, the chocolate chip cookie was invented.

1933 1935 1937 1939 1941 1943 1945

- Adolph Hitler becomes leader of Germany
- Prohibition ends
- First drive-in movie
- Nylon is invented
- First Heisman Trophy
- First helicopter flight
- FDR is reelected
- Amelia Earhart disappears
- First ballpoint pen
- Great Britain and France declare war on Germany
- First McDonald's
- FDR is reelected
- Mount Rushmore is finished
- Japan attacks Pearl Harbor and the U.S. declares war
- U.S. tests first jet
- D-Day
- FDR is reelected
- FDR dies

Find the F.D. Roosevelt stickers on sticker page C.

33 HARRY S TRUMAN

President from 1945–1953

By the time he was fourteen, Harry S Truman had read every book in his town's library. But what did the "S" in his name stand for, you ask? Not a thing. Because his parents couldn't decide which grandfather to name him after (Shippe or Solomon) they left his middle name just plain "S."

Elizabeth "Bess" Truman
Bess and Harry Truman went to the same school from the fifth grade on. At the White House, Bess, Harry, and their daughter Margaret were together so much, the staff called them "The Three Musketeers."

Truman was so far behind in the polls in 1948 that one paper went ahead and printed that his opponent had won. Boy, were they surprised when Truman came out ahead!

1884 - 1972

In 1945, Truman made the decision to drop two atomic bombs on Japan. One day later, Japan surrendered and World War II was over.

No new states were admitted.

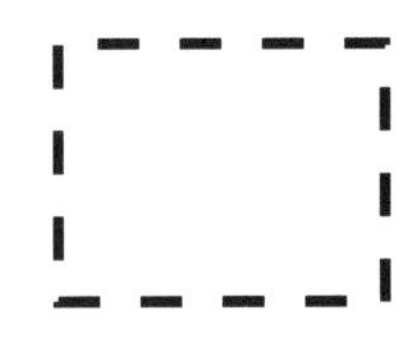

In 1946, the first computer, ENIAC, was introduced. No laptop—this thing weighed thirty tons!

In 1952, Truman gave the first televised tour of the White House.

1945 1946 1947 1948 1949 1950 1951 1952 1953

- 1945: World War II ends; The United Nations is formed
- 1947: Jackie Robinson becomes the first black major league baseball player
- 1948: First Polaroid camera; Truman orders desegregation of U.S. Armed Forces; "Cold War" officially begins; Truman is elected
- 1949: First nonstop round-the-world flight
- 1950: Korean War begins
- 1951: First color TV show

Find the Truman stickers on sticker page C.

DWIGHT D. EISENHOWER

President from 1953–1961

As the Supreme Commander of the victorious armies in Europe, General Dwight David ("Ike") Eisenhower was so popular after World War II that *both* political parties asked him to run for president!

Mamie Doud Eisenhower
As an army officer's wife, Mamie Eisenhower moved 27 times in 37 years. Her eight years in the White House were the most she'd spent in one place since her marriage.

What did Ike like? Golf was his favorite sport, but he also liked to paint, and set up an art studio in the White House.

1890 - 1969

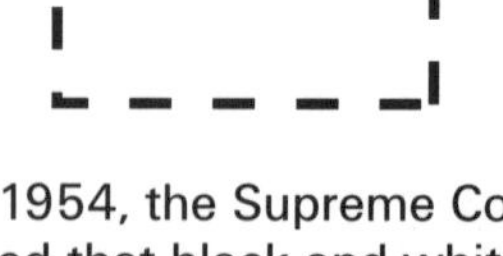

In 1954, the Supreme Court ruled that black and white children could no longer be forced to go to separate schools.

Alaska and *Hawaii* became states—and there were fifty!

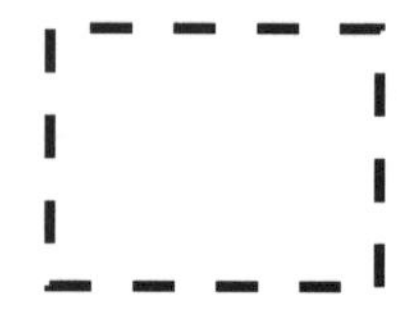

In 1955, Disneyland opened.

In 1957, the Soviet Union got a head start on the space race by shooting the satellite *Sputnik* into orbit

1953
- First 3-D movie
- Korean War ends

1954
- First atomic power plant
- Elvis Presley records his first song

1955
- First televised presidential news conference
- Rosa Parks, a black woman, is arrested for not giving up her bus seat in a "whites only" section

1956
- Eisenhower is reelected

1957
- Eisenhower sends troops to make sure a public school in Arkansas admits black students

1958
- First American space satellite launched

1959
- First 7 U.S. astronauts are picked

1960
- First aluminum cans

Find the Eisenhower stickers on sticker page C.

JOHN F. KENNEDY

President from 1961–1963

At 43, John Fitzgerald Kennedy was the youngest president ever elected—and the youngest to die. His assassination shocked the country and is still a mystery—since the suspect, Lee Harvey Oswald, was killed before he could go to trial.

Jacqueline Bouvier Kennedy
Jackie Kennedy worked to make the White House into a historic and cultural showplace. Of course, she's probably best remembered for her stylish "Jackie look," which women around the world tried to copy.

1917 - 1963

Kennedy was the first Boy Scout to become president.

No new states were admitted.

JFK declared that the torch of government had passed to a "new generation of Americans," and urged young people to "Ask not what your country can do for you—ask what you can do for your country."

Also in 1961, Alan Shepard became the first American to go into space—three weeks after the Soviet Union's first man.

In 1961, in Germany, Communist East Berlin and free West Berlin were officially divided by the Berlin Wall.

1961
- Peace Corps is founded
- U.S. sends first chimpanzee into space

1962
- John Glenn becomes the first American to orbit the earth

1963
- Martin Luther King, Jr., leads Freedom March to Washington D.C.
- JFK is assassinated

Find the Kennedy stickers on sticker page C.

LYNDON B. JOHNSON

President from 1963–1969

Lyndon Baines Johnson wanted to build a "Great Society" for all Americans, regardless of their color or how much money they made. But his years in office saw a divided society instead...divided over the Vietnam War...divided over civil rights...and, of course, divided between "hippies" and the "establishment."

Claudia "Lady Bird" Johnson
A nurse gave Lady Bird Johnson her nickname on the day she was born, when she told her parents that she was "as purty as a ladybird." Johnson proposed to her on their very first date.

"LBJ" weren't just Johnson's initials—they were also the initials of his wife and daughters (Lynda Bird and Luci Baines), his Texas ranch, and his dogs, Little Beagle Johnson and Little Beagle Junior.

1908 - 1973

LBJ liked to give guests to his ranch ninety mile-per-hour tours in his favorite Lincoln Continental.

No new states were admitted.

In 1967, the Green Bay Packers beat the Kansas City Chiefs in the very first Super Bowl.

By 1968, the Vietnam War had made Johnson so unpopular, he announced that he would not run for reelection.

1963
- Two days after JFK's assassination, Jack Ruby shoots suspect Lee Harvey Oswald

1964
- The Beatles "invade" the U.S.
- Congress gives LBJ power to use military force in Vietnam
- LBJ is elected

1965
- First space walk
- Civil rights riots in Los Angeles
- First miniskirt

1966
- National Organization of Women is founded

1967
- First human heart transplant
- LBJ appoints the first black Supreme Court justice—Thurgood Marshall

1968
- Martin Luther King, Jr., is assassinated
- First U.S. astronauts orbit the moon

Find the L.B. Johnson stickers on sticker page C.

RICHARD M. NIXON

President from 1969–1974

Richard Milhous Nixon was the first president to visit all fifty states, and the only one to resign from office. If he hadn't stepped down, he might have been the first president to be impeached for his part in the scandalous Watergate break-in.

Patricia Ryan Nixon
Pat Nixon met her husband at tryouts for a play at a local theater. Not only did they each get the part—but Nixon proposed to her that very day.

Nixon played a mean game of poker—and it's said he won enough while he was in the Navy to pay for his first political campaign.

1913 - 1994

In 1972, five men were arrested for breaking into Democratic party headquarters in the Watergate Hotel in Washington D.C. At first Nixon said he knew nothing about it. But audiotapes later showed that he had.

No new states were admitted.

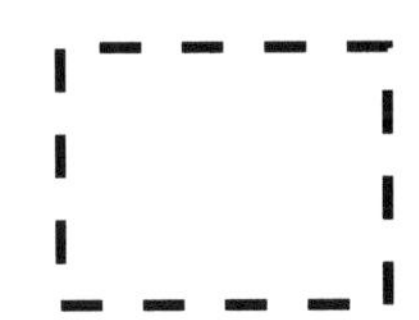

In 1969, Neil Armstrong and Edwin Aldrin became the first men to walk on the moon.

Also in 1969, the original Woodstock music festival was held.

1969
- *Sesame Street* debuts

1970
- First Earth Day
- World Trade Center is built

1971
- 26th Amendment lowers the voting age from 21 to 18
- Nixon becomes the first president to visit China and Moscow

1972
- Last U.S. combat troops leave Vietnam
- Nixon is reelected in a landslide victory

1973
- Sears Tower is built
- Vice President Spiro Agnew resigns after he is charged with taking bribes
- Gerald Ford is named the new vice president

1974
- Little League is opened to girls
- Congress begins Nixon impeachment hearings
- Nixon resigns

Find the Nixon stickers on sticker page D.

38 GERALD R. FORD

President from 1974–1977

Gerald Rudolph Ford got to be president in a most unusual way: First he was appointed by President Nixon to replace Vice President Agnew, who had been forced to resign. Then, when Nixon was himself forced to resign, Vice President Ford suddenly became President Ford!

Elizabeth "Betty" Ford
A former dancer and model, Betty Ford was a very popular first lady who actively supported women's rights. She's also known for the Betty Ford Clinic for alcohol and drug dependency, which she founded after she left the White House.

Ford was a football star in college, and was even offered contracts by professional teams. Instead, he went to Yale Law School, where he made extra money as the football coach and as a model.

1913 -

In 1976, the U.S. celebrated its Bicentennial—the 200th birthday of the Declaration of Independence!

No new states were admitted.

In 1976, *Viking 1* became the first U.S. spacecraft to land on Mars.

Ford's daughter, Susan, had her senior prom in the White House.

1974 ***1975*** ***1976***

- Vietnam War officially ends
- U.S. and Soviet ships link in space
- Two failed assassination attempts are made on Ford's life
- First VCR

Find the Ford stickers on sticker page D.

39 JIMMY CARTER

President from 1977–1981

Jimmy Carter tried to make the White House a more informal, comfortable place. He did away with trumpet fanfares, carried his own bags, and built his daughter, Amy, a tree house on the White House Lawn.

Rosalynn Smith Carter
Both Rosalynn and Jimmy Carter tried to set good examples for the American people. During the energy crisis, they kept the heat so low in the winter, Rosalynn had to wear long underwear around the White House.

Before getting into politics, Carter ran his family's peanut farm in Georgia. His very first job was selling boiled peanuts on the streets when he was five.

1924 -

Carter was the first president born in a hospital.

No new states were admitted.

In 1978, Carter helped negotiate the historic Camp David Peace Accord between long-time enemies Egypt and Israel.

In 1980, Mount St. Helens in Washington State erupted. It was the first volcano to blow up in the U.S. since 1921.

1977 **1978** **1979** **1980** **1981**

- 1977: First personal computer
- 1978: First test tube baby
- 1978: First transatlantic balloon crossing
- First Walkman
- 1979: Three Mile Island nuclear power plant accident
- Over 60 Americans are taken hostage at the U.S. embassy in Iran
- First Rollerblades
- 1980: U.S. boycotts Summer Olympics in Moscow to protest Soviet invasion of Afghanistan
- Mission to rescue hostages in Iran fails

Find the Carter stickers on sticker page D.

RONALD REAGAN

President from 1981–1989

A former actor, Ronald Reagan was so good at using television to get his ideas across to the people, he earned the nickname "the Great Communicator." He was also the first president to wear contact lenses.

Nancy Davis Reagan
Ronald and Nancy Reagan met in Hollywood, where she was acting in movies too. They made only one movie together—*Hellcats of the Navy*.

1911 -

Reagan was the only professional actor to become president. He made 53 movies before he moved on to politics.

Reagan liked to keep a jar of his favorite food—jelly beans—on his desk. He also liked to read newspapers from around the country every morning—comics first!

No new states were admitted.

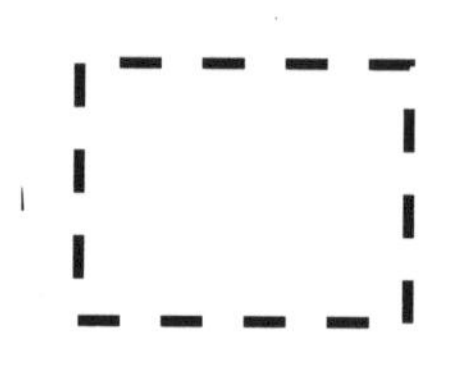

In 1981, the space shuttle made its first flight—and became the world's first reusable spacecraft.

In 1983, the first CD players were sold.

1981
- Hostages in Iran are released
- John Hinckley, Jr., shoots and wounds Reagan and three others
- MTV debuts

1982
- Reagan appoints the first female Supreme Court justice—Sandra Day O'Connor
- First artificial heart implant

1983

1984
- Reagan is reelected

1985
- The *Titanic* is found

1986
- The space shuttle *Challenger* explodes
- Iran-Contra scandal is exposed

1987
- First snowboard

1988
- U.S. and U.S.S.R. agree to reduce nuclear weapons

Find the Reagan stickers on sticker page D.

GEORGE BUSH

President from 1989–1993

George Bush was the first sitting vice president since Martin Van Buren to run for and win the presidency. And he was only the second president to have a son who also became president.

Barbara Pierce Bush
Barbara Bush might be the only first lady to have a World War II bomber named after her. When George was a pilot in the Navy, he named his airplane in her honor.

"Read my lips: No new taxes!" was Bush's motto during his campaign—but it was "Read my lips: No more broccoli!" after the election. Bush hated broccoli so much, he had it banned from all White House menus.

1924 -

In 1990, the Bushes' springer spaniel Millie "wrote" a best-selling book (with a little help from Mrs. Bush).

No new states were admitted.

In 1991, the U.S. declared war on Iraq. Six weeks later, Iraq surrendered and Desert Storm, as the war was called, was over.

In 1990, East and West Germany were reunited, the Berlin Wall was broken down—and Bush soon declared the Cold War over.

1989 — Exxon *Valdez* spills 10 million barrels of oil off the Alaskan coast

1990

1991 — First laptop computer

1992 — 500th anniversary of Columbus's voyage to America

1993

Find the Bush stickers on sticker page D.

42 BILL CLINTON

President from 1993–2001

William Jefferson Clinton was the first president to be born after World War II. Because of personal scandals, this popular president was the second president to be impeached by the House of Representatives. However, the Senate decided that he should not be removed from office.

Hillary Rodham Clinton
Hillary Clinton stopped practicing law when she moved to the White House. In 2000, she became the first First Lady to be elected to the U.S. Senate.

1946 -

Clinton was the only president to play the saxophone on TV. And in high school, he played in a jazz band called the Three Blind Mice.

No new states were admitted.

Clinton and Vice President Al Gore were the first running mates to campaign across the country in a bus.

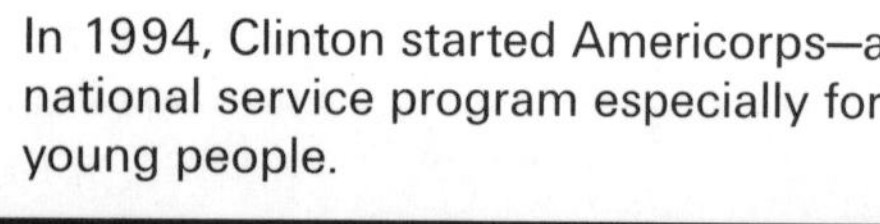

In 1994, Clinton started Americorps—a national service program especially for young people.

In 1995, the Million Man March drew African American men from across the country to Washington D.C.

1993
- World Trade Center is bombed
- Whitewater investment scandal is exposed

1994
- Woodstock II music festival
- Leaders of Israel, Palestine, and Jordan sign peace agreements
- Baseball strike begins

1995
- Baseball strike ends
- Federal Building in Oklahoma City is bombed

1996
- Clinton is reelected

1997

1998
- At age 77, John Glenn, who orbited the earth in 1962, flies another U.S. space mission
- The House impeaches President Clinton

1999
- Michael Jordan retires from the Chicago Bulls

2000
- Vladimir Putin is elected President of Russia, succeeding Boris Yeltsin

Find the Clinton stickers on sticker page D.

GEORGE W. BUSH

President from 2001–

George W. Bush is only the second president to have a father who has also served as president. The second President Bush says that as a kid he dreamed about being a professional baseball player. In one of the closest elections in the history of the United States, it took many weeks to confirm that Mr. Bush was the winner.

Laura Welch Bush
Laura Bush grew up in Midland, Texas, where friends introduced her to George W. Bush in 1977. They were married just three months later. Laura Bush was a public school teacher with a master's degree in library science.

1946 -

George W. Bush was the first president to be elected in the twenty-first century.

No new states were admitted.

Thanks to the Internet, millions of people around the world can communicate daily with each other!

George W. Bush and a group of investors once owned the Texas Rangers baseball franchise.

Find the G.W. Bush stickers on page D.

THE WHITE HOUSE

Although George Washington picked the place, chose the design, and drove in the first stakes for the White House, he never got to live there. His term ended before the house was ready. John Adams and his family had the honor of being the first first family to live in the mansion, and Thomas Jefferson was the first president to spend his whole term there. (Jefferson also submitted a design for the house when a competition was held in 1792—but he lost to a young architect named James Hoban.)

Until the Civil War, the White House was the biggest house in America. This is just some of what you'll find there:

132 Rooms
32 Bathrooms
12 Chimneys
147 Windows
412 Doors
7 Staircases
3 Elevators
6,000 Visitors per day

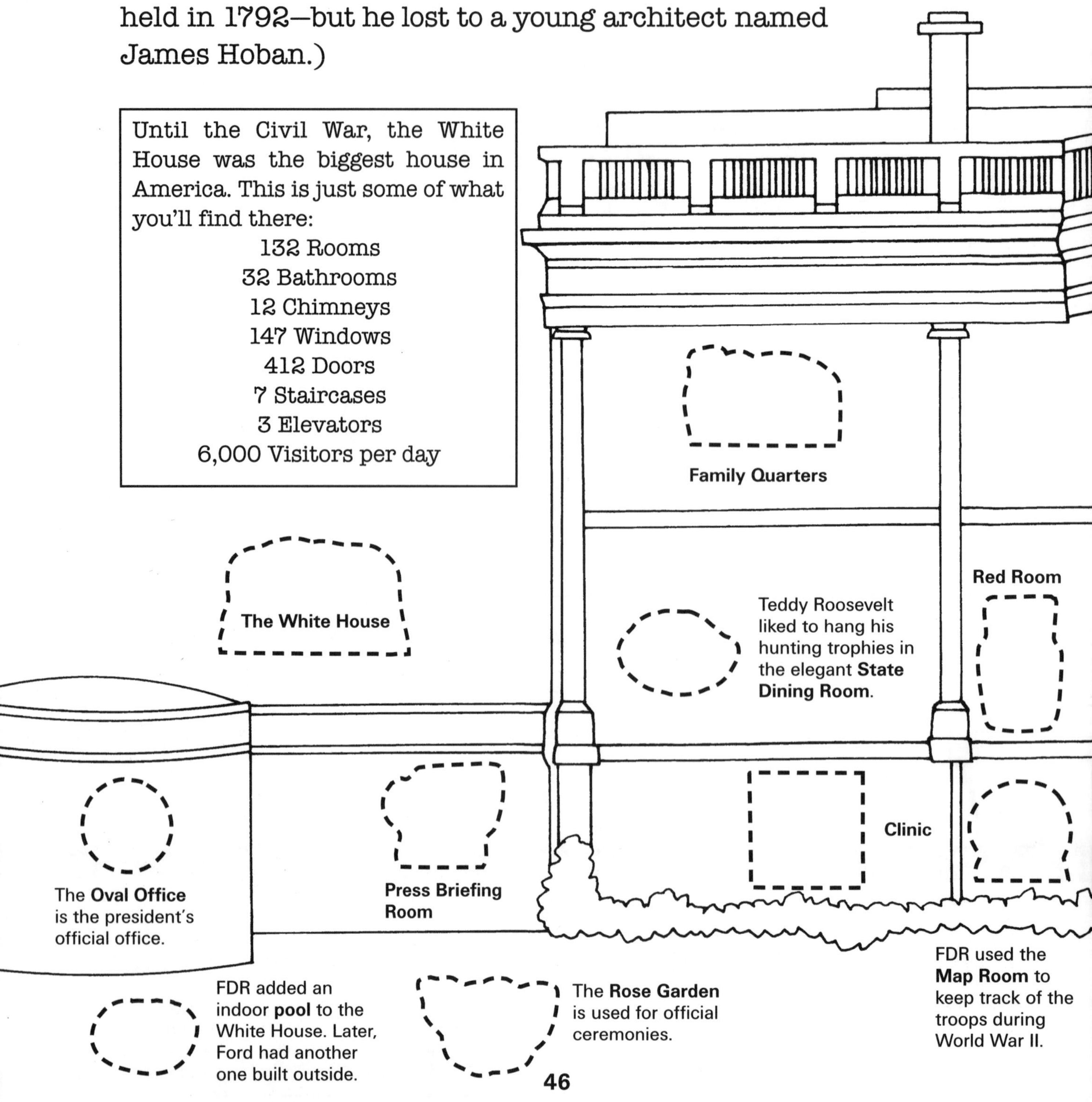

The White House wasn't always called the White House. In fact, it wasn't always white! When it was first built, it was tan. But no one ever called it the "Tan House." Some called it the "President's House," others the "Executive Mansion." Some even called it the "Presidential Palace." Then when Jefferson moved in, he had the outside whitewashed. But it wasn't until Madison had the mansion rebuilt and repainted, that people began calling it the "White House." Teddy Roosevelt finally made the name official in 1901.

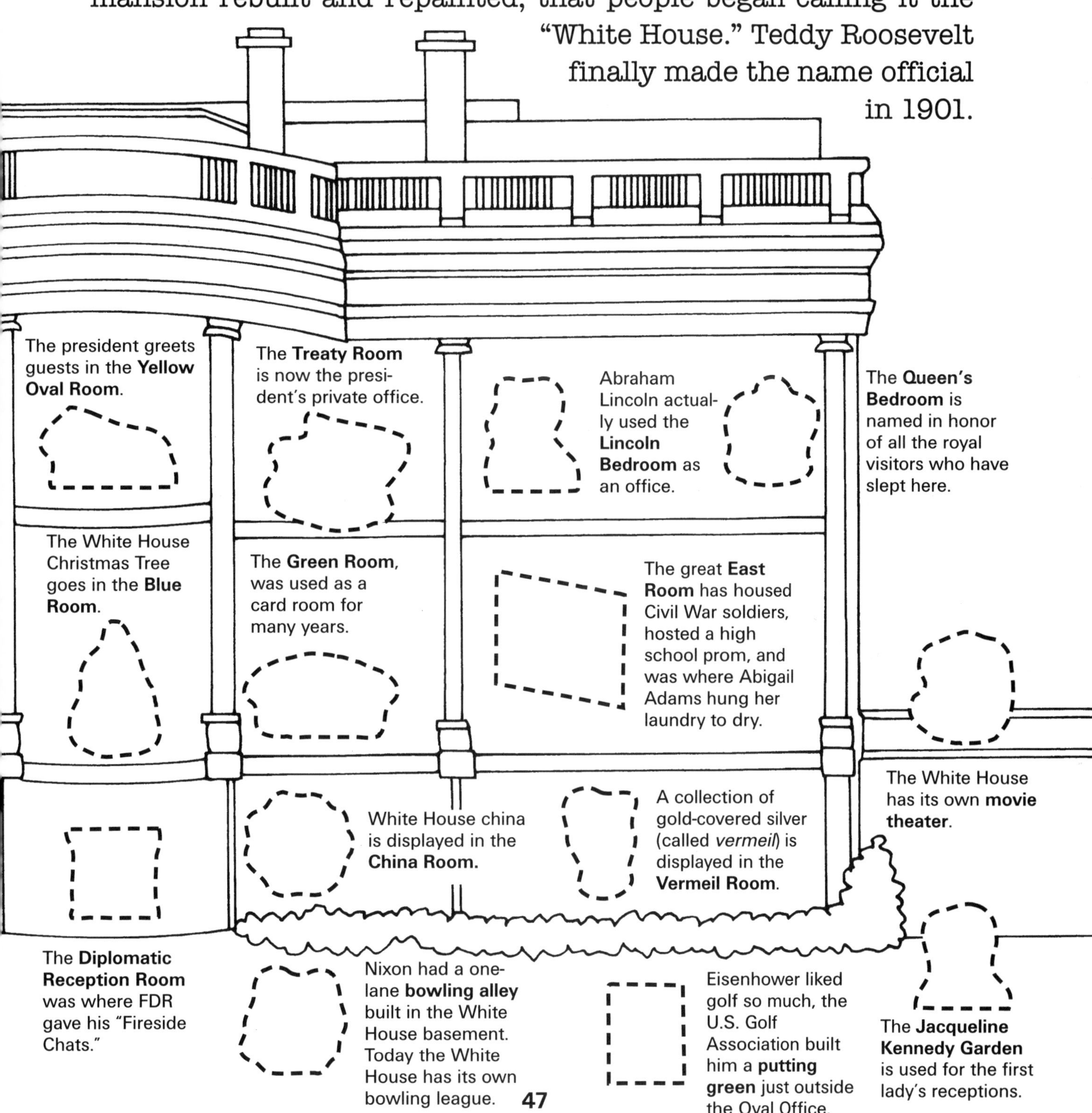

BOO!

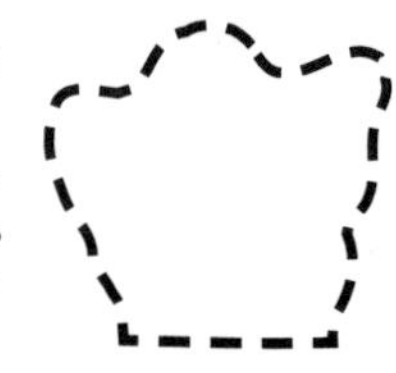

You know the White House is full of history—but some people say it's also full of ghosts. Mary Todd Lincoln said she saw the ghost of her son Willie at the foot of her bed, and the ghost of Andrew Jackson, too!

Certain rooms are said to be haunted. Some say the ghosts of Jefferson and Tyler haunt the Yellow Oval Room. And during the Truman administration, a guard there heard a voice whisper, "I'm Mr. Burns, I'm Mr. Burns...." David Burns was the original owner of the land around the White House—and had not been happy to give it up.

When Queen Wilhelmina of the Netherlands visited in the 1940s, she was visited by Lincoln's ghost in the Queen's Bedroom (then called the Rose Room). The queen heard a knock on the door, opened it...and there he was! Naturally, she fainted.

DEAR MR. PRESIDENT....

Is there something you'd like to ask the President?

Write a letter!
You can send it to the president at home:

The White House
1600 Pennsylvania Avenue
Washington, DC 20500

Or send an E-mail message:

PRESIDENT@WHITEHOUSE.GOV

You can find out a lot more about the presidents, too, by checking out the White House home page on the World Wide Web:

HTTP://WWW.WHITEHOUSE.GOV